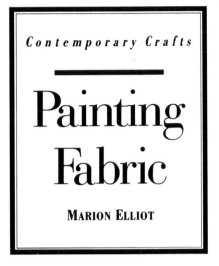

Contemporary Crafts

Painting Fabric

MARION ELLIOT

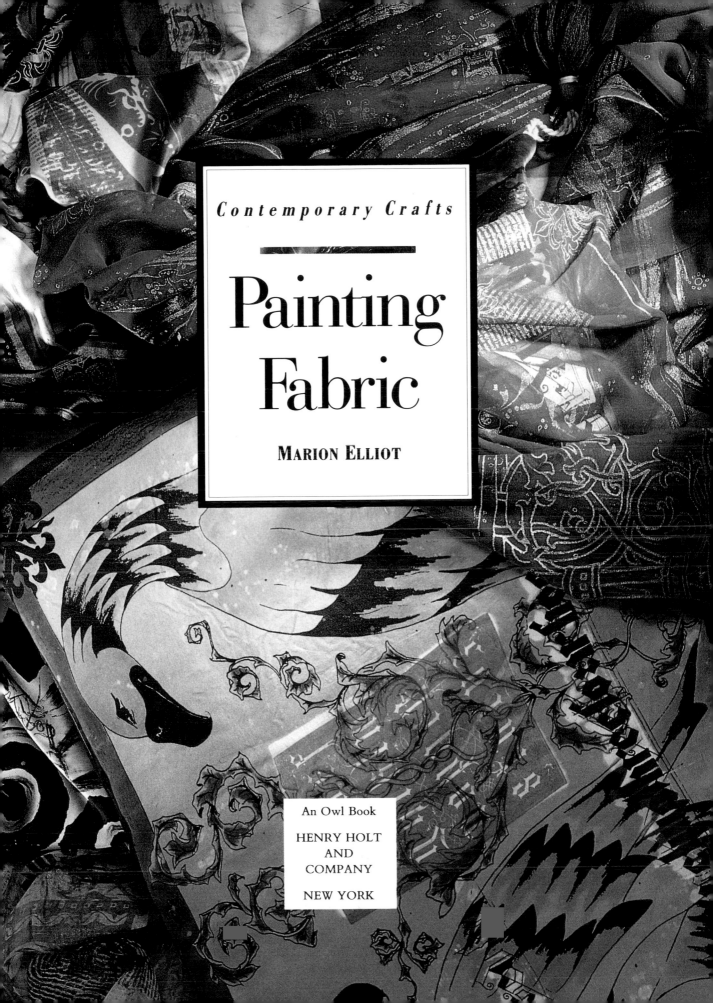

Contemporary Crafts

Painting
Fabric

MARION ELLIOT

An Owl Book

HENRY HOLT
AND
COMPANY

NEW YORK

Henry Holt and Company, Inc.
Publishers since 1866
115 West 18th Street
New York, New York 10011

Henry Holt® is a registered
trademark of Henry Holt and Company, Inc.

First published in the United States in 1994 by
Henry Holt and Company, Inc.
Published in Canada by Fitzhenry & Whiteside Ltd.,
195 Allstate Parkway, Markham, Ontario L3R 4T8.
Originally published in Great Britain in 1993 by
Charles Letts & Co. Ltd.
An imprint of New Holland (Publishers) Ltd.

Library of Congress Catalog Card Number:
94-76066

ISBN 0-8050-3324-6

Henry Holt books are available for special promotions and premiums.
For details contact: Director, Special Markets.

First American/Owl Book Edition—1994

Designed and edited by Anness Publishing Limited, London
Editorial Director: Joanna Lorenz
Editor: Penelope Cream
Art Director: Tony Paine
Designer: Roy Prescott
Photographer: Steve Tanner

Printed and bound in Spain

1 3 5 7 9 10 8 6 4 2

CONTENTS

INTRODUCTION

THE SUMPTUOUS art of fabric painting is an ancient craft practised worldwide. Its long tradition in Europe can be traced from the richly painted cloths of medieval times which were often used as wallhangings in imitation of the beautifully worked extravagant tapestries that adorned the walls of castles and great houses.

This tradition of using hand-painted cloth in interiors became very popular and continued well into the nineteenth century when it was still common to find huge numbers of decorated silks, velvets and wools in both European and American homes.

In 1601, the East India company was formed in England to create trade links with India and the Spice Islands, and large quantities of painted cloths began to appear in Europe. Known as 'pintadoes', these cloths were a forerunner of wallpaper, and were sold as wall coverings.

Another innovation in gracious living was the introduction in the seventeenth century of carpets. Prior to this, loose straw and then circular straw mats had sufficed, but Persian and Turkish carpets were gradually appearing, although only in the homes of the wealthy. Just as painted cloths imitated more expensive tapestry wallhangings, carpet substitutes were found. Known as floor cloths, these were mats made of cotton or canvas, and decorated with oil paint in a variety of motifs including flowers, animals and geometric arrangements.

One of William Morris' block-printed cotton designs, 'Lea', produced in 1912.

. . . .

Curtains were seldom seen at windows until the seventeenth century, and again only in the homes of the wealthy. Much more popular were hand-painted roller blinds made of cotton or silk which protected furnishings from strong sunlight and afforded some privacy. Common decorative treatments included landscapes and *trompe-l'œil* effects. So great was their popularity that there were still firms devoted solely to blind-painting in the nineteenth century. There was also a great demand for hand-decorated blinds in America.

The Industrial Revolution of the eighteenth century fundamentally changed the manufacture of textiles in England. Inventions such as the flying shuttle and the spinning jenny meant that cloth could be woven much more quickly, and, of course, in far greater quantities. The mechanization of the printing industry occurred at the same time. Since the Middle Ages material had been block-printed by hand, and the images individually and laboriously coloured in, but now engraved copper plates could print a square yard of fabric in one movement. The subsequent introduction of roller printing changed textile manufacturing from a cottage industry to one of mass production.

Fabric printers now employed artists to churn out hundreds of new textile designs each year. This led to a gradual deterioration of quality in draughtsmanship and design, and the loss of traditional skills. This decline disturbed the hugely influential artist and craftsman William Morris, and others of the Arts and Crafts Movement, who felt that mass production resulted in decorative art that was spiritually

A fine example of a Nigerian Yoruba adire cloth; the fabric is decorated with cassava-paste resist designs applied with a chicken feather and then dyed deep blue with indigo dye.

. . . .

dead. Morris favoured a return to a simpler, more sympathetic approach to design reminiscent of that of the Middle Ages, when ornament had a meaning and a purpose. His criticisms led to a revival of interest in less ornate, more 'homely' textiles and furniture, and a respect for the hand-produced. Where hand-painted cloths had once been regarded as a cheap substitute for tapestries and carpets, they were now seen as superior to the mechanically woven, readily available textiles that had flooded the market with their harsh dyes and brash designs.

Echoing the spirit of the Arts and Crafts Movement, the Wiener Werkstätte opened in Vienna in 1903 to make and sell the best in modern design and craftsmanship. This 'applied arts' branch of the Vienna Secessionists, presided over by Gustav Klimt, produced a wide variety of hand-painted and hand-printed fabrics, mostly pongee silks, from 1905 onwards.

With similar ideals, although employing a more avant garde execution, the Omega Workshops were founded in London in 1913 by the art critic Roger Fry to produce furniture, pottery, textiles and rugs. Hand-painted textiles were an important element of the Omega style and were designed for both clothes and furnishing fabrics.

Although painted fabrics were often too labour intensive to produce on a commercial basis in large numbers, artists such as Enid Marx and Phyllis Barron carried on the ideals of the Arts and Crafts Movement in their work, making wooden blocks and hand-printing their own fabric. Modernism was an important force in fabric design, and many fine artists produced textiles which, although mechanically printed, retained a painterly, spontaneous quality. This is especially apparent in the textiles of Zika and Lida Ascher who supplied lengths of fabric to couturiers such as Christian Dior and Pierre Cardin. During the 1940s the Aschers collaborated with artists such as Feliks Topolski, Graham Sutherland and John Piper to create beautiful and bold silk squares that are, in effect, paintings on silk.

Beyond Europe, hand-painted textiles have existed from the earliest times. Fabric painting flourished in India and China for many centuries, with both countries producing exquisitely beautiful paintings on silk. Wallhangings and scrolls were a speciality and arrived in Europe as part of a huge influx of Chinese goods during the mid-eighteenth century. This was the age of Chinoiserie; the Chinese style so delighted Western eyes that silk, pottery and other goods were painted to order for export to Europe.

The Chinese silk painters were responsible for a great innovation, the invention of 'gutta', a thick paste that, when used to paint the outlines of a design onto fabric, blocked its mesh. This created barriers that prevented different colours from running into each other. This technique was also widely used in Japan, especially for kimono paints, and eventually spread to European textile painters.

The Japanese were extremely accomplished fabric painters, and raised the technique to an art form of considerable beauty. At one time, many high-ranking men and women wore silk garments hand-painted with gold and silver pigments, as did Samurai warriors. In Tibet, silk and hemp banners were painted with Buddhist imagery by temple painters, and were hung around shrines. They depicted deities in the main, although some paintings were secular, of domestic subject matter. The Indonesian countries were also producers of beautiful, richly patterned and very distinctive hand-painted fabrics. The Balinese used pigments made from natural substances such as soot and earth to paint directly onto lengths of cloth, sometimes embellishing them with gold and silver.

One of the best-known decorative fabric techniques, batik, comes from Indonesia. This involves applying hot liquid wax to fabric before and during dyeing, in order to resist colour. This hugely versatile and distinctive technique is still practised today, although large quantities of machine-produced 'batik-effect' fabric are exported each year.

Another form of wax resist is practised by the Bambara women of Mali to produce intricately decorated cloth called 'bokolanfini'. The cloth is dyed before painting in a leaf and bark solution. A mud paste is used to decorate the cloth with symbolic designs, and is eventually rubbed off to reveal beautiful bright white drawings on a dark background. A similar process is used by the Yoruba of Nigeria, who stencil fabric with a dye-resisting cassava paste, and colour the cloth with indigo to reveal white patterns on a blue-black background.

Nowadays, of course, hand-painted fabrics are something of a luxury, with their own special quality that is lacking in mass-produced cloth. Hand-painted fabrics are too costly to produce commercially except in small, exclusive runs, and the advent of the silk screen has made it possible to achieve a hand-painted effect far more quickly and cheaply. However, fabric painting is practised increasingly today by a large number of artists who enjoy the freedom, spontaneity and sheer versatility of the medium, and the development of simple-to-use fabric paints, from silk colours to puffy pens, has made it possible for many more people, often working at home, to experience the excitement and satisfaction of making clothes or soft furnishings from cloth painted to their own design.

A twelfth-century example of Chinese silk painting using inks and fine detail.

MATERIALS AND EQUIPMENT

THE MATERIALS and equipment needed for fabric painting are readily available from specialist shops, and some artists' suppliers. The basics are listed below; individual projects detail specific cloth, paints and equipment.

FABRICS

The projects in this book use a variety of fabrics, from denim to velvet. Only 100 per cent pure, natural fabrics are used, as synthetics and synthetic mixes take paints differently and the results are unpredictable. When selecting a fabric it is important to consider its eventual function, and to choose a suitable type and weight of cloth. For example, thin silk is not an ideal choice for furnishing fabric, and heavy calico would make a rather cumbersome scarf!

For beginners, light- to medium-weight habotai silk is a good choice. It is relatively inexpensive and has a smooth surface which is perfect for painting. It comes in a wide range of colours, and is often available with hand-rolled edges, or made up into silk squares. It is a versatile fabric, ideal for scarves, shirts, wallhangings and so on. Heavier silks, such as crêpe-de-chine, have beautiful draping qualities, and are especially suitable for lingerie and gowns. There are many other silks available in various weights, and with differing characteristics. Choose the one with qualities that most appeal to you. Several different pure cottons are available, from light-weight, finely woven cambric to heavy-weight calico. Many of the techniques detailed in this book, such as stencilling and printing, may be successfully carried out on most weights of cotton; experiment first on a scrap of fabric to check that fabric and technique are compatible.

BRUSHES

A selection of brushes is needed for fabric painting. Fine, medium and thick brushes, both pointed and flat, may be used to produce a variety of different marks on your fabric. It is a good exercise to paint with each brush on white paper first, to explore the range of effects which can be achieved. Brushes specifically for fabric painting are available and are very long-lasting, but good-quality watercolour brushes are a good alternative. Chinese calligraphy brushes are also suitable. Brushes should be cleaned thoroughly after use. Wash them in warm water with a little soap, rinse them thoroughly until the water runs clear, squeeze out the excess, and then re-shape the hairs between finger and thumb. Never use hot water to clean your brushes - it will melt the glue around the ferrule, causing the hairs to fall out.

FABRIC PAINTS

The popularity of fabric painting has meant that there is a bewilderingly wide variety of textile paints available, a consequence of manufacturers' attempts to develop safer, easy-to-use paints that do not require fiddly steaming or baking to make them permanent. It is strongly recommended that only water-based non-toxic iron-fixable paints, pigments and guttas or outliners are used, and that attention is paid to the manufacturer's instructions before use. Some colours may spread more than others so it is a good idea to test each type on a scrap of fabric before painting. The basic iron-fixable paints, which are available in most ranges, are as follows:

WATER-BASED SILK PAINTS: these are free-flowing intensely coloured paints suitable for use on all silks and, usually, thin cottons. They may be thinned with water, and mixed within each range to create a wide variety of colours. They are light-fast and washable once iron-fixed. Some may also be mixed with a special silk medium to make pastel shades.

WATER-BASED PERMANENT FABRIC PAINTS: these are thicker, non-spreading paints that can be used on natural fabrics. They are suitable for most applications, including paints, sponging and stencilling, and are iron-fixable. These paints come in basic flat colours, metallics, fluorescents and opaques, and are fully intermixable.

HELIZARIN BINDERS AND PIGMENTS: certain iron-fixable fabric pigments should be suspended in a white creamy substance called helizarin binder. The pigments and binder must be mixed together before use. The usual ratio is one part pigment to approximately 10 parts binder, although this may be adjusted to create more or less intense colours – check the manufacturer's instructions first. If you use these pigments and binders, it is important to ensure you have adequate ventilation.

WATER-BASED GUTTAS AND OUTLINERS: these liquids are used to apply the outlines of a design to cloth before it is painted. They clog the mesh creating barriers so that silk paint cannot spread unchecked over the fabric. Gutta may be transparent, in which case it is washed out after fabric has been iron-fixed; it also comes in a variety of colours, including metallics, which are permanent and form

an integral part of the design. Coloured gutta may be applied on top of painted fabric for additional decorative effect.

FABRIC-PAINTING FRAMES

Pinning fabric onto a wooden frame makes painting much easier, as it raises the cloth off the work surface. For some techniques, such as painting, it is an essential piece of equipment. Frames come ready-made in a variety of sizes, and some are adjustable. It is also possible to make simple wooden frames at home from soft wood measuring approximately 5 cm x 1.25 cm (2 in x ½ in). Join the corners with mitre or T-joints, and seal the wood before use.

The fabric should be slightly larger than the frame, and held in place with three-pronged silk pins or fine map pins. If you are painting an item with finished edges, for example a hand-rolled silk square, use dressmakers' fine, single-pronged pins to minimize pin holes.

Once the fabric has been painted, it should be allowed to dry thoroughly, preferably overnight, before the frame is moved or placed in an upright position – wet paint may run otherwise, or dribble over the top of gutta outliners.

FABRIC PENS

A variety of non-toxic fabric pens and crayons is available: the pens may be used in the same way as felt-tip pens to draw directly onto cloth. These come in a range of effects including puffy, shiny, fluorescent and glitter as well as the more usual matt shades.

VANISHING FABRIC MARKERS

PENCILS AND PENS: a soft lead pencil may be used to lightly trace your design onto fabric or, alternatively, you can use a vanishing fabric marking pen. This produces a line that fades automatically after a couple of weeks.

TAILOR'S CHALK: a triangular block of compressed powder usually light blue or cream in colour, may be used to mark fabric. Its edges should be kept sharp to ensure fine, accurate lines. The chalk eventually brushes off and leaves no trace.

STENCIL CARD AND FILM

Stencil card and clear acetate stencil film are available from most artists' suppliers. The card is orange and has a 'waxy surface. Stencil film is transparent, and is useful if you are stencilling a repeat, as you can see through the film to gauge the distance between patterns. Stencil card and film should be cut on a plastic cutting mat with a craft knife. Remember to cut away from you, and mind your fingers! You can also buy pre-cut stainless steel stencils in various designs from specialist shops.

STENCIL BRUSHES

These are short, stubby brushes with very dense, flat-cut bristles. They are used to dab on paint through stencils, and can be used to achieve a mottled effect or a dense block of colour. Synthetic or natural sponges and fabric pens are also good for applying stencilled designs.

SILK-SCREEN FABRIC PRINTING

Silk screens for fabric printing can broaden the range of effects achievable. Screens and squeegees are relatively inexpensive and are available in all manner of sizes.

Before starting to print, your screen, printing surface and washing-out area must be prepared. To prepare the screen, cut four lengths of 5 cm (2 in) gummed paper-strip (two the length and two the width of the screen). Wet the gummed strip thoroughly and stick it along the flat outer side of the screen covering the line where the mesh meets the frame. This prevents the ink seeping under the frame when printing. It also creates a reservoir at the top and bottom of the frame to contain the ink.

SCISSORS

It is a good idea to keep a pair of scissors specially for cutting fabric; do not blunt them by cutting paper and card.

PALETTES

Paints should be mixed on a white surface so that the colour is not distorted. You can buy china palettes from artists' suppliers; old saucers or small bowls make a very suitable alternative.

STEAM IRON

FINE MAP

PURE COTTON

THREE-PRONGED SILK

PURE SILK

CLEAR ACETATE

PENCIL

RUBBER GLOVES

SCISSORS

MASKING TA

GUMMED PAPER TAPE

GLOSSY, FLUORESCENT AND
PUFFY FABRIC PENS

FABRIC PASTELS

FABRIC MARKERS

WOODEN FRAME

CHALK

HELIZARIN BINDER

HELIZARIN PIGMENTS

CRAFT KNIFE

GUTTA APPLICATOR

SILK PAINTS

METALLIC GUTTA

COTTON BUDS

PAINT BRUSHES

FABRIC PAINTS AND PALETTE

SQUEEGEE

BASIC TECHNIQUES

IT IS A GOOD IDEA to protect your work surface with heavy plastic or PVC (American cloth) before you begin. Fabric painting can be quite messy at times. Protect your clothes with a large apron.

COMPOSITION AND DESIGN

Before you start painting your fabric, it is a good idea to work through your design ideas on paper to establish composition and colour. Think about the function of your painted cloth – for example, will it hang in folds? If so, your design should still be easy to 'read' when the cloth is in position. If you are unsure, make a large-scale drawing and mock-up design before you begin. You will achieve more pleasing, harmonious results if you work out your design first, and you will also reduce the chances of making an expensive mistake.

PREPARATION OF FABRIC

It is important to wash lengths of fabric before painting to remove any size that has been added by the manufacturer to improve finish and appearance. Fabric paints will not take evenly on sized material, and ugly patches of colour may appear. Silk may require dry cleaning – check with your supplier first. Washing will prepare pure cotton for use if it is not already pre-shrunk.

TRANSFERRING A DESIGN TO FABRIC

The easiest way to transfer a pattern to fabric is to place the design beneath the cloth and trace over it. If you cannot see the outlines very clearly, draw over your design again with a dark felt-tip pen to make it bolder, and it should show through the fabric. It will then be easy to lightly trace the design

onto the cloth using a soft pencil or varnishing marker pen (which disappears after a few days). Darker fabrics may need to be placed on a direct light source such as a lightbox or against a window before the design can be seen underneath. Tailor's chalk is useful for tracing the design onto darker fabric so that the pattern shows up clearly.

STRETCHING THE FABRIC

Fabric, especially silk, benefits from being stretched before it is painted. This will give a taut, flat surface on which to work. Unstretched cloth is likely to

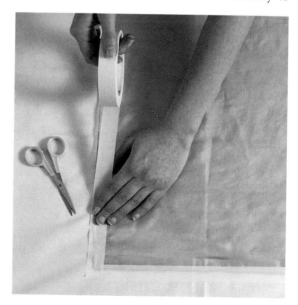

Lay down fabric to be stretched over double-sided tape attached to a flat printing surface and ensure it is taut. Cover the edges with strips of masking tape.

. . . .

sag and collect paint in small puddles, giving unsightly patches of dense colour in the finished design. There are several ways to stretch fabric: items with double layers of fabric such as T-shirts and stockings can be pinned out on a padded printing table with dressmakers' pins, and stiff card slipped between the layers to prevent the paint from seeping through. If you do not have access to a printing table, make a temporary surface by

covering a wooden table or board with a blanket, and then firmly pinning or tacking an old sheet around its edges.

Wooden frames for stretching fabric are also available. They come in a variety of sizes and are square or rectangular. They may be adjustable or static, and are stocked by many craft shops. For small work, a circular embroidery frame can be used. In each case, the fabric should be cut bigger than the frame, and then pinned in place using three-pronged silk pins or fine map pins. Take care to ensure that the grain of the fabric is not distorted during pinning otherwise the painted design will be lopsided when it is removed. The pinned cloth should be taut and springy to the touch.

. . . .

To paint a freehand design, first chalk in your chosen pattern and then fill in with coloured fabric paint.

APPLYING GUTTA OR OUTLINER

Once the fabric has been stretched, it is ready for painting. Since paints run on very fine fabrics such as silk, colours will merge together unless checked. Where clear outlines between areas of colour are required, designs may be traced over first with gutta or outliner, a liquid which blocks the mesh of the fabric and forms a barrier through which the paint cannot pass. Both transparent and coloured gutta are available: it is strongly recommended that the water-based varieties are used. Coloured gutta is permanent, and the lines become an integral part of the design. Clear, water-based gutta can be removed from fabric by washing after the fabric has been iron-fixed.

Gutta is applied in a continuous line from a small metal-nibbed bottle or applicator. The nibs are detachable, and come in three thicknesses. Take care to ensure that no breaks occur in the gutta line or the fabric paint will bleed through. Gutta must penetrate the mesh of the fabric completely in order to block it. Once gutta has been drawn onto stretched silk, turn the frame over and look at the back of the fabric. If adequate liquid has been applied, it should be visible on both sides. Heavy weights of silk may need an application of gutta on back and front in order to create a solid barrier. When gutta application is complete, hold the fabric up to the light. If the painted barrier is solid, without any breaks, the fabric is ready to paint. If there are any holes in the line, re-apply the gutta, and allow it to dry before painting.

If a break in the line goes unnoticed, and paint bleeds through, carefully soak up the excess paint with a tissue, and then gently rub the excess colour from the silk using a small paintbrush dipped in clean water. Allow the fabric to dry, and then repair the gutta line and continue painting.

FREEHAND PAINTING

Fabric paints should be mixed together on a white surface – palettes or old saucers are perfect. Generally, colours may be mixed within the same range – do not try to combine different brands of paint as they may not be compatible. Silk paints may be applied with watercolour, silk or Chinese brushes. As they flow so freely, silk paints should be applied to the middle of each area and pushed gently towards gutta outlines. Cotton buds are useful for applying paint to small areas. Silk and other fine fabrics can be painted freehand for a soft, spreading effect. Use fine brushes for detail and wide brushes to fill in larger areas. With no gutta outlines to impede their progress, the paints will merge to give blurred outlines that can be further softened by stroking the damp fabric with a brush dipped in water.

SPONGING

Sponging is a decorative effect that is used extensively in interior design and pottery manufacture. A natural sponge is used to dab paint onto a surface, and its irregular holes transfer the colour in an interesting and uneven pattern. It is best to use a fairly thick paint for this technique – silk paint is too runny and can spread, blurring the pattern. Sponging can achieve very subtle colour effects if a light paint is dabbed onto neutral-coloured fabric. It can also be used to give startling effects when one colour is sponged on top of a complementary colour, for example, green on red, or blue on orange. Several colours may be sponged one on top of the other to give especially exciting results. Make sure each colour is dry before the next is added, and wear rubber gloves to prevent your hands from becoming stained.

STENCILLING

Stencilling is a traditional decorative technique which uses a shape cut from clear acetate film or paper stencil card. The stencil is positioned onto the fabric, and thick textile paint is applied through the stencil with a sponge or stencilling brush. Fabric pens are also very effective for this technique. The cloth should be fairly closely woven and of medium weight to achieve the best results, as otherwise the paint may bleed beyond the stencil outline. However, it is possible to stencil thin open-weave fabrics such as muslin (cheesecloth) to stunning effect as long as the paint is of the right consistency. Experiment with scraps of fabric first to see if the technique is suitable. Stencilling is very versatile and may be used to make random or repeat patterns. It looks

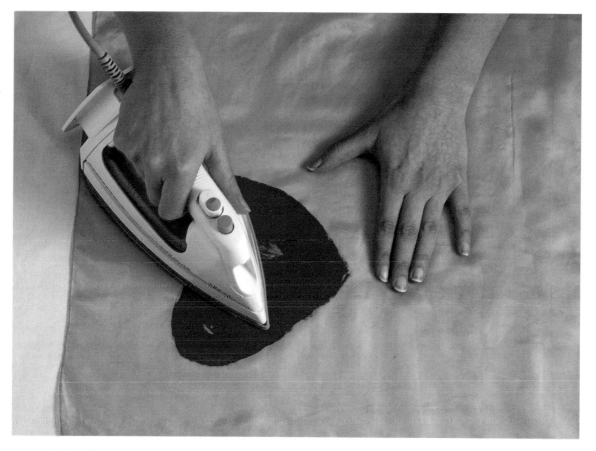

particularly effective when used in conjunction with other techniques, such as sponging, or when embellished with metallic outliners. It is an ideal method for decorating curtain fabric or anything that requires a fairly large repeat, such as bedlinen. An alternative method of stencilling is to cut a design from thin paper and apply it to fabric using a small silk screen and squeegee with water-based fabric pigments.

SALT TECHNIQUE

Salt may be used to create an exciting mottled effect on fabric after paint has been applied. It should be dropped onto cloth while the paint is still wet. The salt absorbs the paint where it falls, creating strange flashes in the colour. Rock salt gives the most dramatic effect because of its large and the varying crystal size. When the fabric has dried, the salt should be thoroughly brushed off and the fabric fixed.

Many fabric paints are fixed and made permanent by heat; one of the easiest and quickest methods of fixing is to use an iron.

. . . .

FIXING FABRIC

Iron-fixable fabric paints are simple to use and do not require any fiddly processes to seal them. When iron-fixable paints are dry, they may be ironed on the reverse side to make them permanent. Different brands of paint may require varying fixing times – check the manufacturer's information for details of time and heat required. It is a good idea to cover fabrics with a cotton cloth before ironing to prevent scorching. When using puffy pens, fix by using an iron on steam setting held a short distance above the fabric without actually touching it.

GALLERY

The variety of work by leading fabric painters is astounding: from practical items on wool and velvet, to swirling wall banners on heavy silk and intricate pieces of jewellery with machine-stitched detail, the items displayed in this section reveal an astonishing range of application, style and technique.

The freehand and printed designs, different weights and types of fabric used and the individual motifs and patterns shown here will provide inspiration and visual stimuli for the new fabric painter. Try experimenting with a variety of patterns taken from your surroundings, nature, fine art and illustration to produce items of your own for both practical and decorative purpose.

~

**Manuscript and
Music Silk**
BETTINA MITCHELL
Bettina uses acid and
procion dyes to hand
paint, print and stencil
silk in all weights. Her
fabrics have great
richness and opulence,
with imagery inspired by
classical music scores and
medieval manuscripts.

Embroidered and Painted Silk

JUDY CLAYTON

Judy Clayton produces subtly coloured garments and accessories painted with protein dyes and metallic pigments. These are often richly encrusted with heavy metallic embroidery in a variety of metallic and cotton threads to create a three-dimensional surface.

. . . .

'Euphrates' Swathe

ISABELLA WHITWORTH

The inspiration for this vivid length of crêpe-de-chine is the embroidery of the Marsh Arabs of Iraq. The design was drawn freehand onto the fabric with gutta, and painted with steam-fixable silk paints.

. . . .

Cat Cushions

DORSE JUKES

These unusual and appealing cat cushions are closer to pieces of fabric sculpture than soft furnishings. They are made from heavy cotton and decorated in a painterly manner with iron-fixable paints. Trapunto quilting is used in conjunction with wadded filling to give each cushion a three-dimensional and life-like effect.

Horse-Theme Scarves

DAMIEN LE BAS

These richly patterned silk scarves are decorated with themes drawn from Damien's experiences of Romany culture. The designs are painted directly onto heavy silk using helizarin binder and pigments.

. . . .

Wool Wraps

TRISHA NEEDHAM

The startling visual effect of placing dense black on top of bright and bold colours is a recurrent theme in Trisha's vibrant scarves and wool wraps. She uses steam-fixed acid dyes to decorate large squares of lightweight wool, rather as a painter might fill a canvas. Her designs are nearly always abstract, usually with geometric symbols or brush-mark details.

. . . .

Floorcloth

NATALIE WOOLF

Natalie's talents as a muralist are evident in the patterned floorcloths she produces in canvas. The designs are applied in oil-based paints in earthy, Mediterranean colours. Her sources of inspiration range from peeling frescoes to the distressed walls of semi-demolished buildings.

. . . .

Duck Cushions

DORSE JUKES

These handsome duck cushions are part of a series inspired by Dorse's interest in natural forms. She draws on her background as a painter and illustrator to decorate her shaped cushions with iron-fixable paints in subtly glowing colours.

. . . .

Decorated Scarves, Hat and Shirt

ANNE TOOMEY

After a degree in Fashion Textiles, Anne Toomey was employed as a textile designer for several years before becoming a freelance artist. She now produces a range of bold hand-painted and printed fabrics and accessories, working with discharge dyes on wool, silk and, most strikingly, on velvet.

. . . .

Silk Clothing and Scarves

VICTORIA RICHARDS

These textiles are produced using a deliberately limited palette of procion and discharge dyes, achieving a great depth of colour and huge variety of hues and tones within the range. Victoria combines hand-painting, printing and over-dyeing to enhance the silks' texture.

. . . .

Ornate Cushions

RUTH PRINGLE

The cotton satin fabric for these elaborate cushions is sponged and stencilled with screen-printing inks to give a mottled, layered effect. Ruth draws inspiration from a variety of sources including heraldry, needlepoint samplers and the architectural decoration and motifs of the Middle East.

. . . .

Animals and Urns

HARRIET CAMERON

Originally a stained-glass artist, Harriet now concentrates on producing scarves, wallhangings and lengths of silk painted with intricate motifs in gutta and steam-fixable paints. Her sources of inspiration include natural forms and geometric designs. She is especially fond of gardens and garden ornaments and has produced a range of fabrics based on a horticultural theme.

. . . .

Wax-Resist Circle Designs

TESSA LAMBERT

Tessa has developed her unusual wax-resist techniques during the past decade using a system of waxing and over-dyeing that produces richly coloured textural effects on silk and wool. She applies wax in layers using very loose brush strokes; the cloth is then coloured using steam-fixable paints.

. . . .

Indian-Inspired Silks

SARBJIT NATT

Sarbjit draws upon her Indian background to produce her own contemporary interpretations of traditional themes. Her work is inspired by a variety of sources including sari borders and the Phulkari and Bagh textiles of India. The fabric is decorated using steam-fixable silk paints and metallic guttas to produce jewel-bright, shimmering geometric designs.

. . . .

Bright Ties and Accessories

FRANNIE

Frannie uses vibrant French silk dyes and gutta to paint her fabrics. She enjoys the freedom of hand painting and its scope for one-off designs. Recent collections have been inspired by the Italian designer Pucci, South American imagery and paintings of the Italian Renaissance.

. . . .

GREETINGS CARDS

SARBJIT NATT

SMALL, BRIGHTLY COLOURED and intricately patterned pieces of hand-painted silk are ideal for greetings cards, each one being an individual and original gift in itself. Large pieces of silk can be marked up and painted at the same time to produce a whole series of designs. Metallic gutta forms a clear and exotic contrast to the shining colours of the silk paints while forming an effective outline for ease of decoration.

~

MATERIALS AND EQUIPMENT

• medium-weight habotai ivory silk • iron • wooden silk frame • three-pronged silk pins or fine map pins • vanishing textile marker • ruler • metallic gutta and applicator • silk paints in a variety of colours • assorted paintbrushes •paper • thin card • spray glue

. . . . . .

1 Wash, dry and press the silk. Stretch onto the wooden frame using three-pronged silk pins or map pins. Make sure the stretched fabric is very tight and smooth with absolutely no wrinkles.

2 Protect your work surface with heavy plastic. Using a vanishing textile marker and ruler, mark up a box approximately 7.5 cm x 10 cm (3 in x 4 in) in size on the silk. Draw a freehand design within the box.

3 Apply metallic gutta along the outlines of the design, using a ruler to obtain a straight line. The gutta will create a solid barrier in the mesh of the silk and prevent the silk paints from merging together. Allow to dry thoroughly.

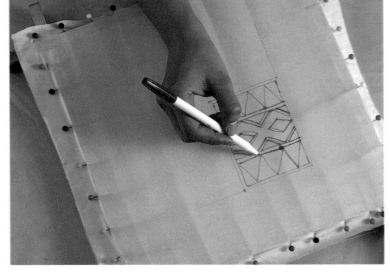

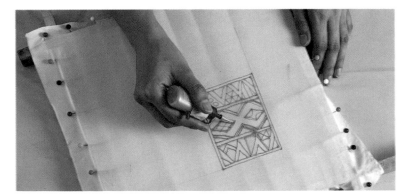

4 When the gutta is completely dry, arrange all your painting equipment. Apply the silk paints, washing the brush in clean water between colours. Leave the fabric to dry thoroughly before removing it from the frame.

5 Place the painted silk between two sheets of clean white paper, and iron to fix the paint according to the manufacturer's instructions.

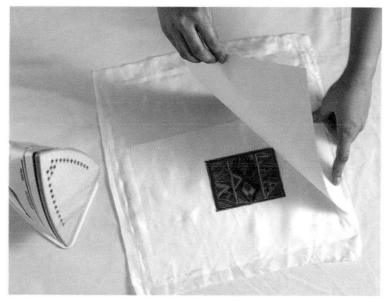

6 Carefully cut along the gutta edge of each painted box. Make sure that you do not leave any white fabric around the gutta borders. To assemble, cut thin card to the dimensions you require for the greetings card. Spray the reverse of the silk design with glue (after first opening all available windows to ensure good ventilation). Stick the silk in place on the front of the card. Smooth out to remove any air bubbles.

BEDLINEN

SUZANNA HOLLAND

THE PATCHY, antique appearance of this beautifully embellished bedlinen is achieved using an ancient decorative technique called frottage. This entails rubbing pigment onto a surface over a textured background to create an uneven, grainy effect. Concrete floors, unplaned wood, pebbled areas and slate floors all make good textural surfaces. If none of these is available, make a 'portable' surface by covering a piece of thin wood with filler in a rough, peaked texture.

~

MATERIALS AND EQUIPMENT

• *pure cotton pillowcases* • *iron* • *thin wood, to fit size of pillowcase* • *all-purpose filler* • *thick card* • *fabric paints in a variety of colours* • *pencil*

· · · · · ·

1 Wash, dry and press the pillowcase. Take a piece of thin wood cut to fit inside the pillowcase. Mix up a bowl of filler and roughly cover the board to make a textured surface, spreading the filler with a small piece of thick card. Allow the board to dry thoroughly.

2 Cover your work surface with heavy plastic. Insert the textured board into the middle of the pillowcase. This will prevent paint bleeding through and staining the second layer of cotton, as well as providing a patterned surface for the design.

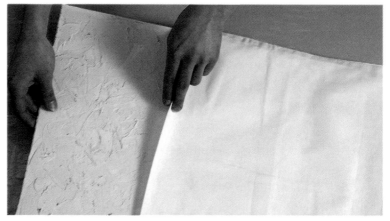

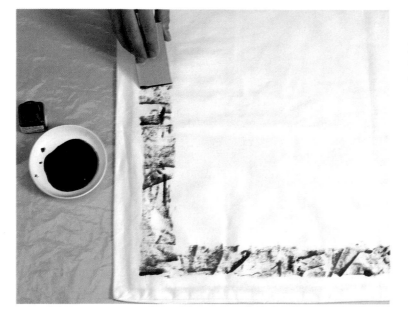

3 Apply the border colour to the cotton using a small piece of thick card, pressing quite hard so that the texture of the board comes through.

4 Using a smaller piece of thick card, decorate the centre of the pillowcase in the same way with a contrasting colour. The smaller the piece of card, the narrower the width of the textured design produced. Continue to build up the design using a variety of different shades and strokes.

5 Add smaller details using the blunt end of a pencil dipped in paint. If you press hard, the texture of the board will show.

6 When the fabric paint has dried thoroughly, remove the cardboard from the inside of the pillowcases and iron them through a length of thin cotton to fix the paint following the manufacturer's instructions. Experiment with matching trims or whole sheets to make a co-ordinating set of bedlinen.

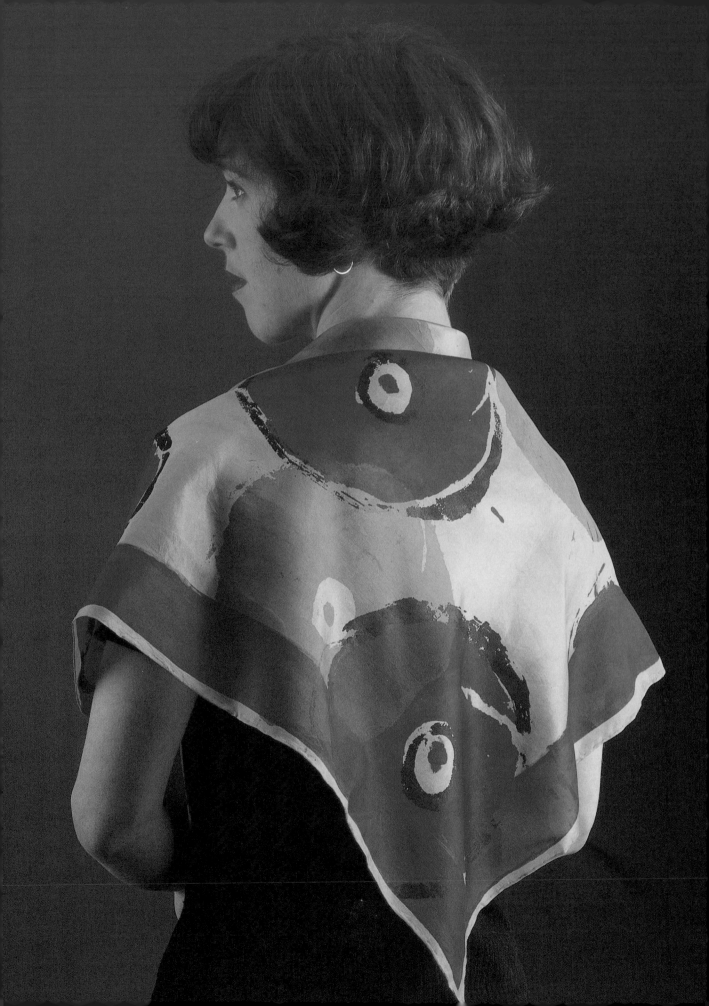

CIRCLE SCARF

VICTORIA RICHARDS

THIS VIBRANT SILK SQUARE is painted freehand with a simple yet highly effective motif that is both chic and casual. The pigments are mixed with a binder before being applied to the silk; this renders the colours opaque and gives them a softness that may be used as a decorative effect. Here, light grey circles are just visible under the more strident red pattern. The paint is applied in a loose, flowing manner using a wide, soft brush. The random nature of the design means that there is no strong diagonal or vertical pattern in the scarf, and it will look good however it is folded or worn.

~

MATERIALS AND EQUIPMENT

• *pre-hemmed silk square*
• *double-sided tape*
• *masking tape* • *tailor's chalk* • *helizarin pigments*
• *helizarin binder*
• *assorted paintbrushes*
• *iron*

. . . . . .

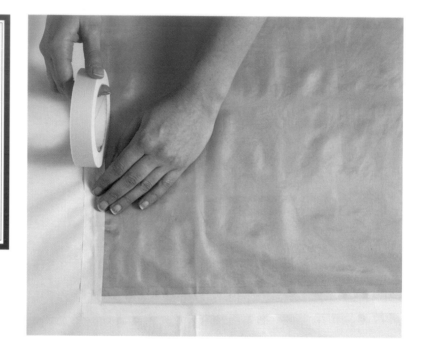

1 To stretch the silk square, lay down strips of double-sided tape and place the silk on top. Secure with a layer of masking tape over the edges of the silk.

2 Lightly sketch out your design onto the silk square using tailor's chalk.

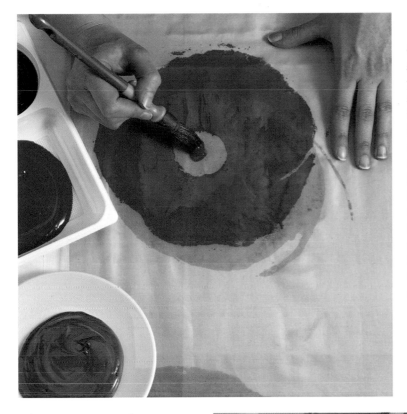

3 Decide on a colour scheme and mix up the pigments. Colours should be mixed by adding one part pigment to 10 parts binder. This ratio may be adjusted by adding more binder for paler shades, or less pigment for darker. Using a paintbrush, apply the pigments to the silk square. It is best to start with the lightest colour and work towards the darkest. Allow each colour to dry thoroughly before applying the next. Make sure the scarf is dry before removing it from the table. Unused pigments may be stored for one month in clean, dry screw-top jars.

4 Fix the pigments by ironing on the reverse side according to the manufacturer's instructions. If the silk feels a little stiff after fixing, pull the material rapidly through your hands several times to soften it, and then re-iron.

DENIM BABY OUTFIT

FREDDIE ROBINS

THE WONDERFUL DECORATIONS adorning this baby outfit are derived from traditional folk art imagery, but are interpreted in a contemporary and witty fashion. The clothes have been painted with a selection of the 'novelty' fabric pens that are now available. These come in a variety of finishes and special effects including fluorescent, glitter, glossy and a spongy, puffy texture that children love.

~

MATERIALS AND EQUIPMENT

• *child's denim dungarees or overalls* • *pencil* • *thin card* • *fine black waterproof felt-tip pen* • *thick cardboard* • *puffy fabric pens in a variety of fluorescent colours* • *glossy fabric pens in a variety of colours* • *iron*

. . . . . .

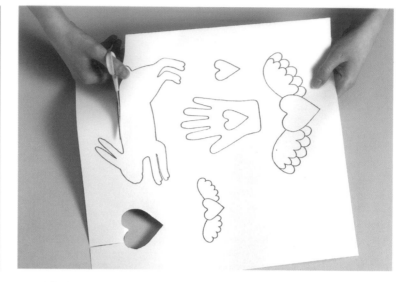

1 Draw your images onto thin card and cut them out. These are your templates.

2 Protect your work surface with heavy plastic. Lay out the garment flat. Place the card templates in position on the fabric and draw around them with a fine black waterproof felt-tip pen.

3 Before starting to paint, insert a piece of thick cardboard inside the dungarees to prevent the fabric paint from bleeding through to the other side of the garment.

4 Re-draw the outline of each image with a coloured fabric pen. Keep the pens vertical when drawing, and have the pen nozzle just above the fabric surface rather than touching it. Fill in each shape with puffy or glossy paints. Allow each colour to dry before painting another next to it to avoid paints bleeding into each other. The front of the outfit must be dry (this should take about 4 hours) before it is turned over and painted on the back.

5 When the designs are completely dry, gently steam areas covered with puffy paint on the right side with a steam iron, following the manufacturer's instructions regarding temperature and duration of steaming. This will cause the paint to puff up to a spongy consistency. Do not allow the iron to come into contact with any of the painted areas but hold it just above the garment.

6 To fix the other designs, turn the clothing inside out and place a piece of thin card between the layers of fabric. Iron on the reverse according to the manufacturer's instructions.

CAMISOLE

JUDY CLAYTON

THE SHEER luxury and beautiful draping qualities of fine silk make it the perfect material for lingerie. This camisole has been painted freehand using wax to resist the dye in some areas, and allowing previous layers of colour to show through with a jewel-like brilliance, reminiscent of stained glass and almost too beautiful to keep covered up! Wax-resist designs are very striking yet simple and quick to produce.

~

MATERIALS AND EQUIPMENT

- *silk camisole* ● *pencil*
- *paper tailor's chalk*
- *cardboard box, to fit inside camisole* ● *three-pronged silk pins* ● *paraffin wax, or a mixture of paraffin and micro-crystalline waxes, or household candles* ● *small saucepan or electric wax melter* ● *scrap of silk*
- *small paintbrush* ● *silk paints in a variety of colours* ● *iron*

. . . . . .

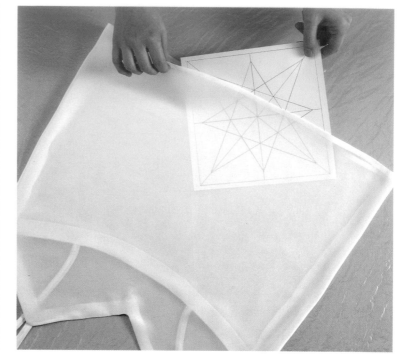

1 Protect your work surface with heavy plastic. Draw your design to size on a sheet of paper. Place the camisole on the work surface and insert the sheet of paper inside it so that the design is visible through the silk.

2 Trace the drawing onto the front of the camisole using tailor's chalk.

3 Cut down the walls of the cardboard box to a height of about 7.5 cm (3 in). Insert the box inside the camisole so that the two layers of fabric are kept apart during painting.

4 To make the silk taut, turn the box over then pin the garment with three-pronged silk pins along both sides so that the fabric is stretched and smooth.

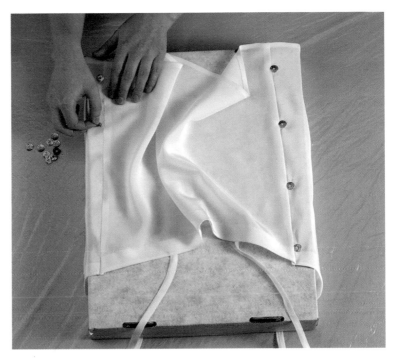

5 Melt the wax. If melting the wax in a saucepan, remember that household candles take longer than the other types of wax to melt. The selected wax should be heated at a low temperature so that it will melt slowly. Do not allow the liquid to bubble, and on no account leave it unattended at any time. When the wax is ready, it will become clear and very fluid. If it becomes too hot, it will smell and begin to smoke - turn the temperature down immediately. When melted, test the wax on a small scrap of silk. If the wax flows easily and leaves a translucent patch on the silk, this means it will have pene-trated the cloth and is ready for use. If the mark left is opaque, the wax is not hot enough, and should be very carefully heated for a few more seconds.

6 Paint the wax onto the front of the camisole following the chalk outline. Use a fairly small brush and apply the wax in single brush strokes. Recharge the brush after each stroke, and apply the wax around the outer edge of the design. Keep a scrap of silk to hand to wipe excess wax from the brush.

7 Paint the silk paints onto the camisole in bands of colour within the wax outlines. Blend each colour into the next, but remember to rinse the brush thoroughly between colours. Allow the fabric to dry.

8 Using tailor's chalk, mark an inner design onto the centre of the painted area. Again, paint wax around the outside line of this new design.

9 Fill in the centre of the second wax area with a contrasting colour silk paint. Allow the painted areas to dry thoroughly before removing the camisole from the box.

10 To remove the wax from the silk, place the camisole between sheets of plain white paper. Place a generous amount of paper underneath the camisole, to protect the back of the garment. Heat the iron to just above silk setting, and iron over the top sheet of paper. The wax will melt and come through the paper. Remove the paper and repeat the process several more times until no more wax appears. Dry clean the camisole to remove any stiffness and slight residue of wax.

HAIR CLIP

SARBJIT NATT

SILK IS THE PERFECT compliment to long, glossy hair, and is particularly suitable to be made into a subtly glowing hair clip. Metallic gutta is used to draw the design onto the silk before it is painted. The gutta is both functional and decorative: it forms a barrier which prevents the individual colours from running into each other, and is also an integral part of the design, creating a delicate golden framework that is reminiscent of stained-glass leading.

~

MATERIALS AND EQUIPMENT

• *heavy-weight ivory habotai silk* • *iron*
• *wooden silk frame*
• *three-pronged silk pins or fine map pins* • *hair clip fitting* • *black felt-tip pen*
• *tracing paper* • *masking tape* • *vanishing textile marker* • *metallic gutta and applicator* • *silk paints in a variety of colours* • *paper tissue* • *assorted paint-brushes* • *paper* • *heavy cardboard* • *rubber-based glue* • *thin foam rubber*
• *fine braid* • *epoxy resin glue*

. . . . . .

1 Wash, dry and press the silk. Stretch it onto the wooden frame and hold in position with three-pronged silk pins or fine map pins. Make sure that the stretched fabric is absolutely taut and smooth with no wrinkles.

2 Protect your work surface with heavy plastic. Measure the hair clip fitting and draw a design in black felt-tip pen onto tracing paper, allowing for a generous border around the design. Attach the tracing paper design onto the stretched silk with pieces of masking tape at each corner.

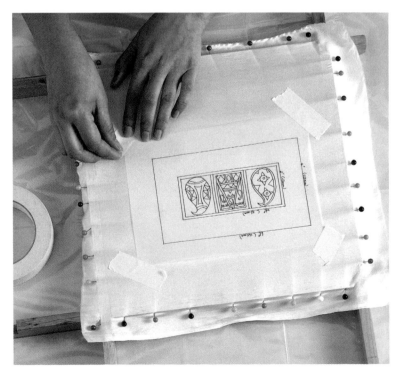

3 Turn the silk frame over over onto the tabletop so that the design is visible through the fabric and so that you have a firm surface on which to draw. Using a vanishing textile marker, trace the design onto the fabric.

4 Turn the screen over once again and apply metallic gutta along the outlines of the design. This will block the mesh of the silk and prevent silk paint from bleeding across and merging. Allow the gutta to dry thoroughly.

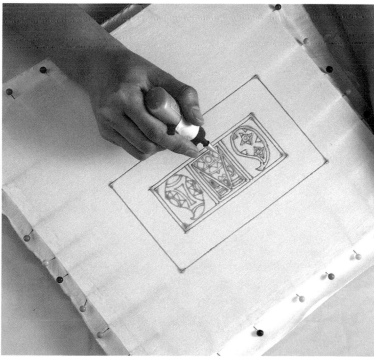

5 Arrange all your painting equipment. Apply the silk paints taking care not to cause any splashes. Colours from the same manufacturer are completely intermixable within each range. Paint a plain border of 2.5 cm (1 in) all round the design. Keep a tissue to hand while you work to mop up any excess paint from the brush. Rinse brushes thoroughly before each change of colour. Small patches of colour or mistakes can be removed using a fine paintbrush or cotton bud dipped in clean water. Alternatively, cover any minor blemishes by adding more paint to create a deeper colour. Allow the fabric to dry before removing it from the frame.

6 Place the painted silk face down between two sheets of clean white paper, and iron it according to the manufacturer's instructions to fix the paint.

7 To assemble the hair clip, cut two pieces of heavy cardboard to the dimensions of the finished design, excluding the plain border. Fix together using rubber-based glue and leave under a heavy object to dry for 24 hours. Glue on a piece of thin foam rubber using the same adhesive and leave to dry for 30 minutes. Trim the edges to fit the cardboard.

HAIR CLIP

8 Cut neatly around the silk design. Place the block on the back of the silk, with the foam touching the fabric. Make sure that it is placed squarely on the painted area. Apply rubber-based glue to the long ends of the cardboard block and stretch the silk over firmly. Glue the ends around the foam, one side at a time. Trim the corners of the short ends and glue these in the same way, making sure that the ends are neat. Leave to dry.

9 Cut a piece of silk slightly smaller than the block and stick it on the back of the hair clip to cover the joins and neaten the edges. Trim the edges with fine braid. Bend the block between fingers and thumbs to shape it into an arch that can be fastened onto the metal hair clip fitting. Remember to have the painted side outermost. Glue the block to the fitting using epoxy resin glue. Follow the manufacturer's instructions carefully regarding mixing and drying times. Hold the block in place with masking tape while the glue dries.

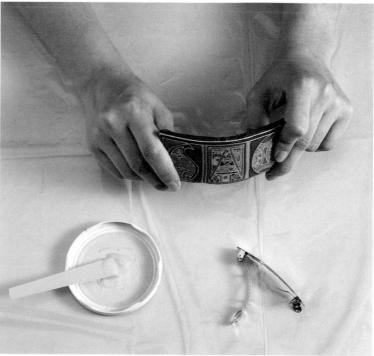

FLOWER T-SHIRT

DELAINE LE BAS

THIS T-SHIRT is decorated using an ingenious and simple technique that combines painting with printing. Fabric paint is applied directly to an acetate sheet with a brush; the texture of the brushstrokes is preserved, giving the resulting print a spontaneous, painterly feel. It is possible to add finer detail to the painted acetate using a pencil before printing. The technique is closely related to mono-printing, and every print will be different. The acetate sheet is held in place with masking tape along one side of the T-shirt so that each separate colour may be registered easily. This makes it simple to apply a final black overlay, for example, or to add a second layer of colour if the first is too patchy.

~

MATERIALS AND EQUIPMENT

● *pre-shrunk pure cotton T-shirt* ● *large sheet of white paper* ● *masking tape* ● *clear acetate* ● *fabric paints in a variety of colour* ● *assorted paintbrushes* ● *iron*

. . . . . .

1 Protect your work surface with heavy plastic before you start. The T-shirt should be printed on a flat surface – a well-covered table is ideal. Place a large sheet of white paper inside the T-shirt: this will prevent the fabric paints from marking the second layer of fabric. Hold the shirt in place on the printing surface with small pieces of masking tape.

2 Place a sheet of clear acetate on the front of the T-shirt. Position it where you want the design to be, and then secure it firmly down the left-hand side with a strip of masking tape. This will allow you to register each new colour before it is printed.

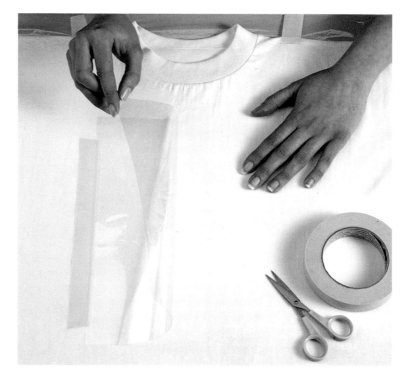

3 Work out your design roughly on paper first, especially the colour scheme. Although acetate printing is a very spontaneous and free way of applying fabric paint, it is a good idea to do a little preparation first. Apply the first colour to the acetate, and press it down gently onto the T-shirt. Each colour is painted separately onto the acetate and printed; the faint outline of each printed colour that is left behind will allow the next colour to be painted on in the right position. Wash brushes thoroughly in clean water before each subsequent colour is added.

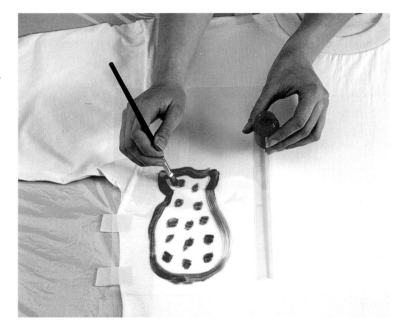

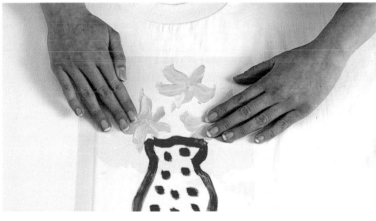

4 Repeat the printing process for the next colour. Try changing brush sizes to achieve a varied effect.

5 When the design is finished, carefully remove the sheet of acetate and allow the T-shirt to dry thoroughly. Remove the paper from inside the shirt. To fix the fabric paint, iron the T-shirt on the front through a piece of paper following the manufacturer's instructions.

EVENING SCARF

JUDY CLAYTON

LUXURIOUS VELVET has been used as the base fabric for this evening scarf. Different coloured pigments have been dabbed through paper stencils to give a mottled 'antique' effect that is both rich and classically elegant. Iron-on paper is used to make the stencils, rather than the more conventional card, metal or acetate; the paper may be positioned with great accuracy, and fusing it temporarily to the base fabric ensures a clean, crisp edge to the design. A two-colour design is shown here, but more colours can be added at will.

~

MATERIALS AND EQUIPMENT

• lined velvet scarf • pencil
• iron-on stencil paper
• iron • thick cardboard
• fabric paints in a variety
of colours • stencil brush or
thick paintbrush • needle
and thread

. . . . . .

1 Draw out your stencil design on rough paper. Cut a piece of iron-on stencil paper to the same size as the scarf.

2 Lay the stencil paper on top of your design and, using a pencil, trace through the pattern for the first colour. Using scissors, cut out the design, taking care to cut smoothly without nicks or bumps.

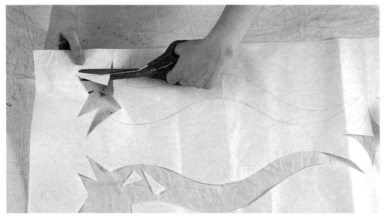

3 Fix the stencil onto the right side of the velvet by ironing according to the manufacturer's instructions.

4 Unpick the end seams of the scarf and slide a large piece of thick cardboard between the velvet and the lining of the scarf to prevent any paint from leaking through. Dab the first colour onto the fabric. Remove the stencil carefully and allow the paint to dry.

5 Draw and cut the stencil for a second colour, and fix onto the velvet as before. Dab on the second shade and remove the stencil from the fabric. Leave the design to dry before removing the scarf from the work surface.

6 Remove the cardboard from inside the scarf. Slip stitch the end seams and fix the design by ironing according to the manufacturer's instructions.

PAINTED TIE

SUZANNA HOLLAND

Silk ties are the perfect vehicles for a statement of style or taste, and hand-painted ties have long featured in the wardrobe of the aesthete and the dandy. The neck-tie may be a splash of colour against a sober grey cloth, or could provide a discreet and elegant compliment to a fine linen suit. Both abstract and figurative designs work well; patterns and images should be designed to fit naturally into the long thin area of fabric available. Specialist suppliers sell blank silk ties for painting and these should be unpicked and ironed flat before decorating.

~

MATERIALS AND EQUIPMENT

- *plain white silk tie*
- *paper • pencil • iron*
- *felt-tip pen (optional)*
- *masking tape • silk
paints in a variety of colours*
- *assorted paintbrushes*
- *pins, needle and thread*

. . . . . .

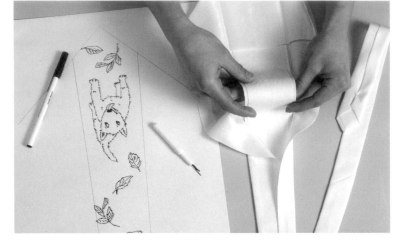

1 Draw out your design to size
on a sheet of paper. Carefully unpick the back seam of the
tie and remove the backing.

2 Iron the tie flat before
beginning to paint.

3 Place the sheet of paper on
your work surface and lay
the ironed tie over it so that the
design shows through. If the
drawing is a little faint, go over
the pencil lines with felt–tip pen.
Fix the tie onto the piece of
paper with masking tape.

4 Using black silk paint and a
small paintbrush, paint in the
outlines of the design, tracing
through the paper onto the silk.

5 Allow the paint to dry thoroughly and then begin to fill in the design with colour. Rinse paintbrushes in clean water before using a new colour.

6 Allow the fabric to dry thoroughly, and then carefully remove the tie from the work surface. Iron the silk on the back to fix the paints according to the manufacturer's instructions.

7 Replace the backing in the tie. Ease it carefully into position so that it will sit flat when the tie is re-stitched. Pin the folded edges of the tie back into place, and slip stitch them together. Take care not to catch the backing as you stitch.

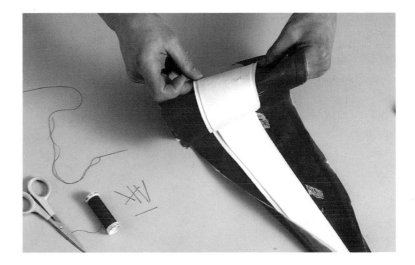

ROLLER BLIND

DELAINE LE BAS

PAINTED ROLLER BLINDS were very much in vogue from the seventeenth century onwards, providing a charming and peaceful focal point for elegant drawing rooms. Today, blinds often replace curtains, and they need not be dull, as this swirling cylinder-printed example demonstrates. Tin cans are opened at both ends, cleaned, and then filled with small amounts of pigment in a variety of colours. When these 'cylinders' are pulled across the fabric from side to side, the paint swirls together and is deposited on the fabric in a marbled effect. Four colours were used in varying combinations for this blind – pick out colours from existing furnishings and combine them to make a complementary blind.

~

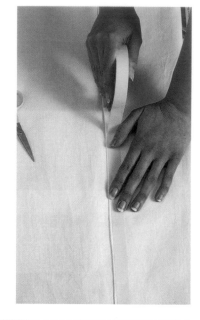

MATERIALS AND EQUIPMENT

• *length of bleached cotton, pre-washed to remove manufacturer's finish (this should be made up before printing to fit a roller blind kit)* • *old newspapers* • *double-sided tape* • *tin cans in a variety of sizes, thoroughly cleaned* • *fabric paints in a variety of colours* • *iron*

. . . . . .

1 Place the washed and ironed cotton on a flat work surface covered with several thicknesses of newspaper. Secure the fabric to the surface with lengths of double-sided tape.

2 Remove the bottom as well as the top of the tin can to leave a metal cylinder. Be careful not to leave any sharp edges. Make sure that the can is scrupulously clean and free from grease before you begin. Carefully place small amounts of three or four colours of fabric paint on the newspaper visible at the bottom of the can.

3 Immediately pull the can across the fabric. The different coloured paints will mix inside the can as it slides across the fabric to produce a swirling marbled effect. When you reach the other side of the blind, continue onto the newspaper; the excess paint will be deposited there without staining the blind.

4 Repeat this process to produce the second band of marbling, using the same (cleaned) can, or another smaller or larger one to give a variegated effect. The wider the mouth of the can, the thicker the band of colour will be.

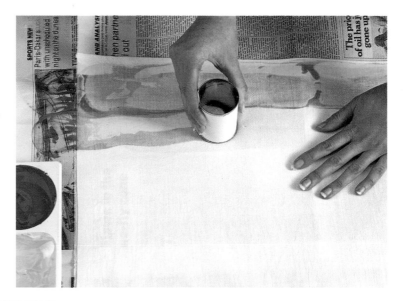

5 Repeat the cylinder printing until the fabric is covered, and then allow it to dry thoroughly. Iron the blind on the reverse through a sheet of paper and following the paint manufacturer's instructions. When the paint is permanently fixed the blind may be attached to wooden rollers from a roller blind kit.

SILK SHIRT

JUDY CLAYTON

THIS DELICATE SILK SHIRT has been decorated with
metallic fabric paints to give a sophisticated and
contemporary look. Metallic paints take on an extra
lustre when applied to silk, and their ease of application
allows for a wide range of experimentation and great
versatility of colour. Freehand patterns may be used to
create single, unique designs, or a traced pattern
repeated on several garments as a hallmark pattern.

~

MATERIALS AND EQUIPMENT

• *silk shirt* • *pencil* • *paper*
• *tailor's chalk* • *cardboard box to fit inside shirt*
• *three-pronged silk pins*
• *silk paints in a variety of metallic colours* • *assorted paintbrushes* • *iron*

. . . . . .

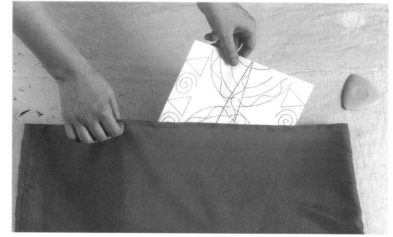

1 Protect your work surface with heavy plastic. Draw your design to size on a sheet of paper. Place the shirt on your work surface, and insert the sheet of paper inside it so that the design is visible through the silk.

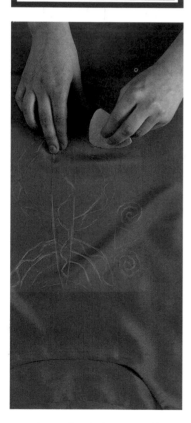

2 Trace the design onto the front of the shirt with tailor's chalk, removing any wrinkles by holding the fabric taut between your fingers as you draw.

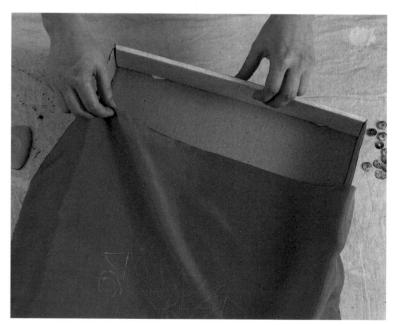

3 Cut down the walls of the cardboard box to a height of about 7.5 cm (3 in) and insert between the front and back of the shirt to keep the layers apart while the paint is applied.

4 To make the silk taut and smooth prior to painting, turn the box over, fold the excess fabric over and fasten down each side with three-pronged silk pins.

5 The design is painted onto the shirt in two layers. First lay down background colours with sweeping textural brushstrokes using a medium-sized brush. Wash the brush in water between each colour. Allow the fabric to dry thoroughly.

6 Add the details of the design in contrasting colours using a fine paintbrush. The paint should be applied with short strokes, and the brush recharged each time. Wash the brush between each colour. Allow the fabric to dry completely before removing the shirt from the box. Iron the reverse of the painted areas to fix the fabric paint following the manufacturer's instructions.

PAINTED STOCKINGS

VICTORIA RICHARDS

BRIGHT PIGMENTS have been used to cover these sunflower yellow stockings with flowers and foliage. The wonderful colours are reminiscent of Provençal fabrics, and are warm and cheerful. Cotton stockings come in a wide range of colours and are the perfect garment for witty, vertical designs. Undyed stockings are also available, and may be dyed to match the base colour of a dress or skirt before painting. Silk stockings can also be used. Thin card should be inserted into each stocking to prevent pigment bleeding through; this will also help to keep the fabric taut and make it easier to paint.

~

MATERIALS AND EQUIPMENT

- *pair of pure cotton stockings* • *cardboard*
- *masking tape* • *tailor's chalk* • *helizarin pigments*
- *helizarin binder*
- *assorted paintbrushes*
- *iron*

. . . . . .

1 Cut the cardboard into simple leg shapes and pull each stocking on, making sure that the material is not twisted and that the fabric grain is straight. Position the heel of the stocking in the centre of the back of the cardboard shape.

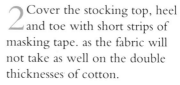

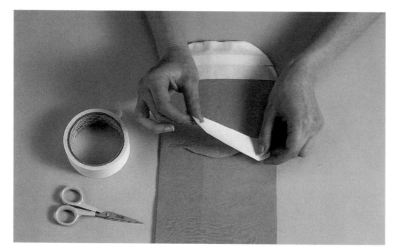

2 Cover the stocking top, heel and toe with short strips of masking tape. as the fabric will not take as well on the double thicknesses of cotton.

3 Decide on your design. It may be helpful to draw it roughly onto paper first. Lightly sketch out the design onto each stocking with tailor's chalk.

4 Protect your work surface with heavy plastic. Decide on a colour scheme and mix up the pigments. Colours should be mixed in the ratio one part pigment to 10 parts binder. The resulting tones may be made darker by adding more pigment, or lighter by adding more binder. Pigments from the same manufacturer can be intermixed to achieve specific colours. Apply the colours, starting with the palest and working towards the darkest. Allow each colour to dry thoroughly before applying the next. When you have finished painting, allow the stockings to dry thoroughly before removing the masking tape and carefully peeling from the cardboard.

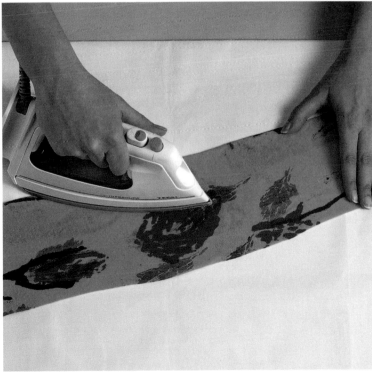

5 Turn each stocking inside out and then fix the pigments by gently ironing the fabric according to the manufacturer's instructions. Rinse the stockings in warm water to remove excess pigment, and re-shape while damp.

CHICKEN CUSHION

FREDDIE ROBERTS

ANIMAL MOTIFS such as dogs, cats and birds have long adorned soft furnishings. This tradition may be very successfully adapted by using such imagery to make shaped cushions where the design is applied to heavy cotton with paper stencils. Traditionally, pigment is dabbed onto cloth with a natural sponge or a stencilling brush through a thin card or steel stencil. Here, the stencilling process is speeded up by using a small silk screen and rubber squeegee. If the thin paper stencil is handled carefully, it may be used several times over to make sets of cushions.

~

MATERIALS AND EQUIPMENT

- *1 m (40 in) washed and bleached cotton* • *pencil*
- *2 large sheets of paper, same size as or slightly larger than the silk-screen*
- *craft knife* • *masking tape* • *fabric-printing silk screen, approximately 50 cm x 65 cm (19½ x 26 in)*
- *green and brown screen-printing fabric ink*
- *squeegee, to fit screen width* • *plastic spatula*
- *coloured fabric pens*
- *black puffy fabric pen*
- *iron* • *washable stuffing (batting)* • *pins, needle and thread*

. . . . . .

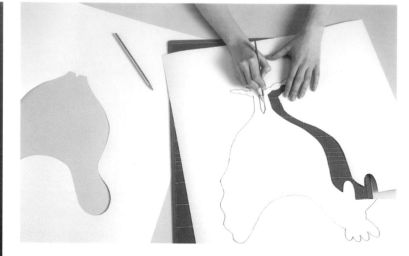

1 To make the first stencil, draw the body of the chicken (minus the feet, beak, comb and wattle) in the centre of a large sheet of paper. Place the paper on a firm surface or cutting mat and carefully cut out the body area using a craft knife. Discard the inner silhouette and keep the cut-out sheet. Place the second sheet of paper under the first and trace around the inside edge of the cut-out body area. Remove the first stencil. Add a beak, comb, wattle and feet to the second chicken shape. Place the sheet of paper on a hard surface or cutting mat and carefully cut out the whole chicken shape using a craft knife. This cut-out silhouette is the second stencil. The surrounding paper may be discarded.

2 Prepare the print surface as directed. Pin or tape the cotton in position, ensuring that the fabric is taut and smooth. Place the first stencil on the fabric close to the selvedge and fix it in position with masking tape. Place the prepared screen on top of the stencil.

3 Wearing rubber gloves to protect your hands from ink stains, pour 100 ml (4 fl oz) brown ink evenly down one edge of the screen into the area that forms the reservoir. Place the squeegee onto the screen behind the line of ink. Hold it at angle of 45 degrees and pull the ink towards you across the screen using a swift, firm motion, pressing down slightly as you pull.

When you reach the other side of the screen pour a little more ink in if necessary, this time in the opposite reservoir. Place the squeegee behind the ink as before, and, again at an angle of 45 degrees, repeat the printing process, this time pushing the squeegee away from you. When you reach the other side of the screen, rest the squeegee against it and carefully lift it off the fabric, removing one side of the screen first, and then the other.

Scrape any excess ink off the screen and squeegee using a plastic spatula. Peel the stencil from the screen. Wash the squeegee and screen immediately after printing and leave them to dry.

4 To print the green border around the chicken, wait until the screen has dried then place the second stencil on top of the printed brown chicken body shape so that it is completely masked. As before, place the screen on top of the stencil. Pour 150 ml (5 fl oz) green ink evenly along one edge of the screen and, again, print twice, adding more ink as necessary. After you have lifted the screen off the fabric, carefully peel the stencil away from the screen.

5 Place the screen onto the other half of the cotton, pour a line of green ink along one side of the screen, and print a plain rectangle of green fabric. This will be used to make the back of the cushion. Remove the screen and clean thoroughly.

6 Allow the chicken to dry thoroughly and then, using fabric pens, colour the beak, comb and wattle. When the ink has dried, outline the body and wings and draw in the chicken's eye with a black puffy fabric pen. Cover the painted and printed areas with a clean pressing cloth and steam the fabric to fix according to the manufacturer's instructions.

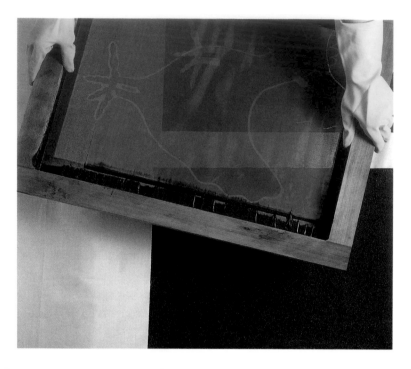

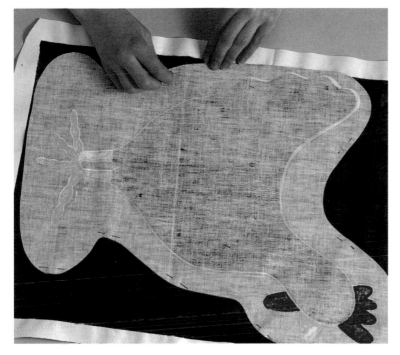

7 Cut around the printed chicken and green border leaving a 4 cm (1½ in) seam allowance. Place the chicken on the green rectangular back and cut around it. Pin the two pieces together, right sides together, and sew, leaving an 8 cm (4 in) opening at the chicken's feet.

8 Clip the curved seam line and then turn the cushion the right way out. Stuff firmly, and slip stitch the opening.

DENIM JACKET

DELAINE LE BAS

THE VERY UTILITARIAN NATURE of the denim jacket and its one-time cult status make it the perfect garment to customize. This method of painting directly onto the fabric gives it a vibrant, homegrown feel reminiscent of folk embroidery. Bleach is applied straight onto the dark blue denim to remove the indigo dye. The resulting white areas are painted with fabric paints in rich, bright colours that stand out beautifully against the dark background. Some areas, such as around the collar and waistband, have been bleached and left blank giving a decorative effect rather like a pony skin pattern.

~

MATERIALS AND EQUIPMENT

• *denim jacket* • *old newspapers* • *thick rubber gloves* • *household bleach* • *cheap bristle brushes for use with bleach* • *tailor's chalk (optional)* • *fabric paints in a variety of colours* • *assorted paint-brushes* • *iron*

. . . . . .

1 Protect your work area from bleach splashes with newspaper before you begin. Stuff the body and sleeves of the jacket with rolled and folded newspaper to prevent bleach soaking through and marking the lower layer of denim.

2 Wearing thick rubber gloves, pour the bleach into a suitable container: a china or glass bowl is ideal but do not use it afterwards for foodstuffs! Open the window to ensure good ventilation. Only paint small areas at a time because of the bleach fumes. Using a cheap bristle brush, start painting your design onto the jacket with the bleach. If you are a little nervous of painting freehand with the bleach, lightly sketch in the design first with tailor's chalk. Leave the jacket for approximately 30 minutes to allow the bleach to react and remove the indigo dye. The denim should be quite white when the bleach has reacted fully. Repeat this process to bleach out the back of the jacket if you intend decorating this too.

3 Once the bleach has reacted and white lines are visible, launder the jacket to remove excess bleach. When the jacket is dry, use a selection of fabric paints to apply colour to the bleached areas. Use a slightly smaller brush than the one that was used to apply the bleach as this will allow a white 'halo' to appear around each colour.

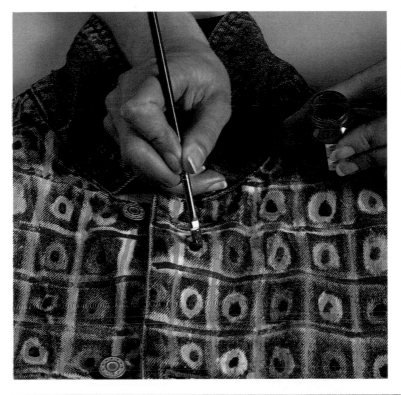

4 Continue building up the
colours until the decoration
is complete. Leave the painted
jacket to dry and then repeat the
process to decorate the back of
the jacket.

5 When the fabric paints have
dried thoroughly, remove
the rolled-up newspaper from
the jacket. Following the
manufacturer's instructions, iron
the reverse of the denim to fix
the design.

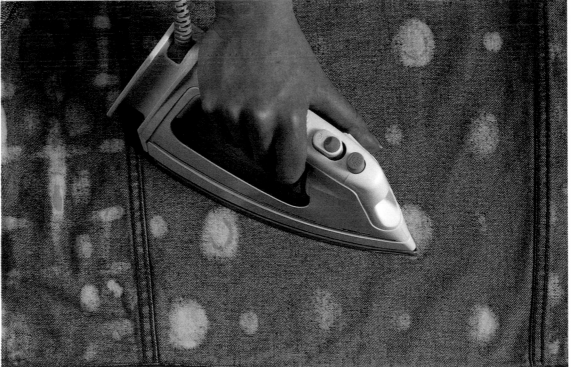

SALT TABLECLOTH

SARBJIT NATT

THE SOFT COLOURS of this silk twill tablecloth are augmented by the application of various types of salt to the wet paint. The salt absorbs the colour in patches, resulting in a mottled, marbled effect that is most unusual. The technique is used here to emphasize the flat washes of colour between the intricately patterned bands of decoration. Gold metallic gutta has been applied on top of salt-treated areas in a freehand design as well as around the lines of the patterned areas: a simple way to add extra richness to fabric.

~

MATERIALS AND EQUIPMENT

• 1 m (40 in) square ivory
silk twill • large wooden
silk frame • three-pronged
silk pins or fine map pins
• vanishing textile marker
• ruler (optional)
• metallic gutta and
applicator • silk paints in a
variety of colours • assorted
paintbrushes • fine- and
coarse-grain salt • iron
• needle and thread

. . . . . .

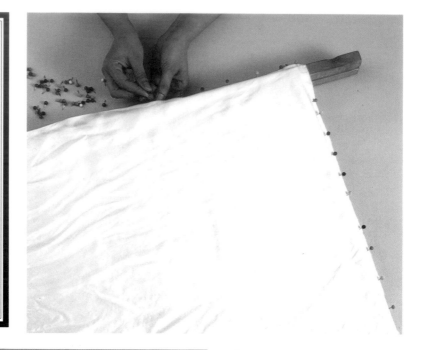

1 Wash, dry and press the silk twill. Stretch onto the wooden frame with three-pronged silk pins or fine map pins. The fabric should be smooth and taut to the touch. Make sure that the grain of the fabric is straight and adjust the pins where necessary.

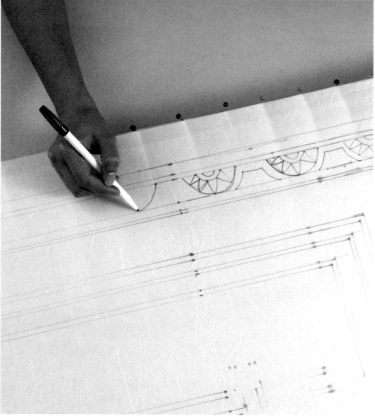

2 Decide on a design and sketch it out on paper first as a guide. Draw in the design onto the silk with a vanishing marker. You may want to use a ruler to draw straight border lines.

3 Protect your work surface with a sheet of heavy plastic. Using metallic gutta in an applicator, draw over the lines of the design. It may be necessary to apply gutta to the back of the fabric as well if the silk is particularly thick. Check to see that the fluid has penetrated right through to the other side of the fabric, and add more if necessary.

4 When the gutta has dried, fill in any solid patterned areas of the design with silk paints. Dot paint into the centre of each area as the paint is very fluid and will spread quickly to the gutta barriers.

5 Apply washes of colour onto the areas of silk where salt is to be used. While the paint is still wet, drop on the salt, adding small amounts at a time. The coarseness of the salt grain will determine the type of pattern produced. You may want to experiment on a spare piece of silk first. As the salt absorbs the paint, the natural colour of the silk will be revealed in places, resulting in strange flashes rather like bleach marks. This effect takes from 30 minutes to an hour to achieve, depending on the type of salt used.

6 When the silk has dried, remove and discard the dirty salt crystals. Draw additional decoration on top of the painted fabric with metallic gutta.

7 Carefully unpin the dry tablecloth from the painting frame, and iron it to fix the paint following the manufacturer's instructions.

8 Trim and roll the raw edges of the tablecloth, and slip stitch the hems into place.

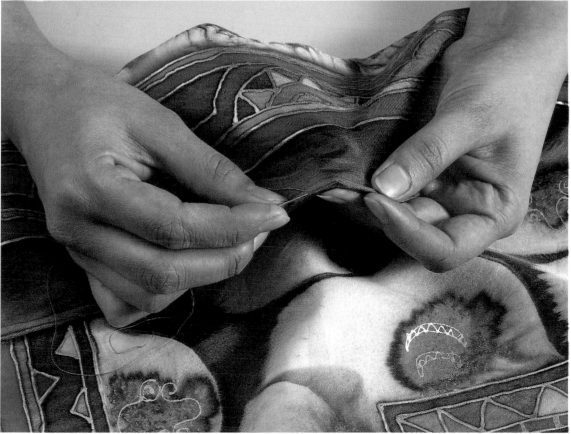

SUPPLIERS

CERULEAN BLUE, LTD., P.O. Box 21168, Seattle, Washington 98111-3168; telephone: (800) 676-8602 or (206) 323-8600. Fabric paints and equipment.

DECART, INC., Lamoille Industrial Park, Box 309, Morrisville, Vermont 05661; telephone: (802) 888-4217. Manufacturer and distributor of about 20 shades of DEKA silk paints and 10 shades of DEKA silk resist and related products. Free catalogue available on request.

EARTH GUILD, 33 Haywood Street, Asheville, North Carolina 28801; telephone: (800) 327-8448 or (704) 255-7818. Distributor of DEKA permanent fabrics, DEKA silk, and DEKA print and FABRIC ART paints, dyes, and other related products. Free catalogue available on request.

RUPERT, GIBBON & SPIDER, P.O. Box 425, Healdsburg, California 95448; telephone: (800) 442-0455 or (707) 433-9577. Manufacturer of JACQUARD fabric paints and silk dyes that are available at stores throughout USA and by mail order from: Artist and Craftsman Supply, Portland, Maine: (800) 876-8076. Commercial Art Supply, Syracuse, New York (800) 669-2787. Dick Blick (catalogue only, no store): (800) 447-8192. Pearl Paint, New York, New York and other stores: (800) 542-522.

ACKNOWLEDGEMENTS

Grateful thanks to Alan Hebden at George Weil &
Sons, Andy Stamatan Hayes, John Godley and
Caroline Banks at Pongees, Tony Atkinson at Sericol,
Dylon International Ltd, and Karen Huntley at Funn
Stockings for their generosity and enthusiasm. Special
thanks to Joanna Lorenz, Steve Tanner and Ben, Neil
for his constant encouragement, and Penelope Cream
for her editing and unfailing good humour and
support. The author and publishers thank the
following for use of photographs: The Bridgeman Art
Library/courtesy of the Board of Trustees of the
V & A (page 6), Jacqueline Herald (page 8) and the
Visual Arts Library (page 9).

INDEX